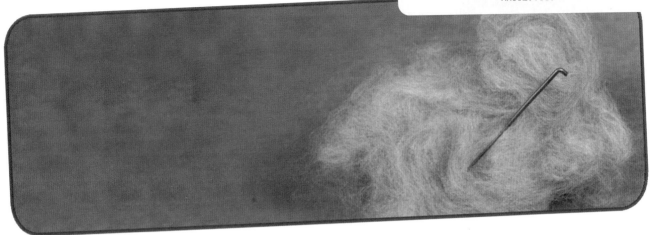

Needle Felting – To the Point

More Needle Felting Techniques
When Things Go Wrong

By

Harlan

This book is dedicated to Toshiko Takaezu
A dear friend – A special artist!

Special thanks to Vicky and Gloria for their invaluable assistance!

All content copyright 2011 by Harlan
All rights reserved.
Do not copy or distribute this information.

Foreword _____ 4
Size – Firmness – Shape _____ 5
    Firmness _____ 9
    Correcting Length _____ 18
    Moving Fiber _____ 22
    Running out of color _____ 25
Introduction to Projects _____ 29
    Winged Mouse _____ 30
    Frog _____ 40
    Squirrel _____ 47
    Gnome _____ 56
    Ferret _____ 67
    Fairy _____ 76
Woodland Diorama _____ 85
    Tree Stump _____ 86
    Door _____ 88
    Tree Roots _____ 91
    Bark _____ 92
    Moss _____ 94
    Plants _____ 97
    Rocks _____ 103
Favorite Resources _____ 107

FOREWORD:

Sculpting with fiber is both a reductive and additive sculpting process.

Unlike sculpting with marble, you are not chipping away and discarding the unwanted excess, you are reducing the volume of the fiber and increasing its firmness and definition. Similar to sculpting with clay, you can easily add more fiber to the sculpture as needed. Being both a reductive and additive sculpting process makes fiber very versatile but also poses some unique problems of control. Control when sculpting with fiber will improve with time and experience.

If you are like me, you still want all the projects you make while you are learning to be successful. The purpose of this book is to not only help you learn the skill of controlling the fiber, but also to show you solutions to the common problems we needle felters face every day.

Now go wash your hands, grab your needles and let's get to work!!

SIZE – FIRMNESS - SHAPE

When sculpting with fiber your main concerns are SIZE, FIRMNESS and SHAPE.

Whatever your project may be, you envision it as having a particular size and shape. Complex shapes are always combinations of simple shapes. A human head reduced to its simplest form is an egg; a leg is a log. If you were making a dog you would want to make all the legs of a similar (if not exact) size.

Fiber for needle felting contains a lot of air. Through the needle felting process you will reduce that amount of air which in turn will allow the scales on the fibers to lock together and become more firm.

How do you measure equal amounts of fiber for parts of your sculpture that will be similar in size?

You could take out a scale and weigh your fiber, but that is hardly a practical solution.

Fiber for needle felting comes in three basic forms. It is either in long drum carded ropes, batting or loose. Drum carded ropes of fiber are almost always completely clear of any vegetable matter that gets incorporated into the wool while on the sheep. Batting may or may not be completely clear of vegetable matter. Loose fiber, being the least processed of the three forms is most likely to contain vegetable matter.

This is drum carded fiber. All of the fibers have been carded into parallel alignment. Some people call this "roving" which technically is not accurate. Roving is wool that has been carded similarly to this, but has also been twisted in preparation for spinning into yarn and is usually found in shorter lengths.

The more accurate name for fiber in this form would be "sliver". I prefer "drum carded ropes". The fiber pictured is Merino which is a fine, lovely wool.

Fiber of this quality is often only used on the surface of needle felted sculptures to save expense.

Needle Felting – to the Point

This wool batting is most commonly used for quilts. Batting prepared specifically for needle felting is more available then it once was, and comes in many colors.

In batting, the fibers are not aligned to run parallel to one another, but the batting is still very consistent in density throughout.

Batting is often sold by size suitable for quilts.

Batting makes excellent "core" fiber, and is used to occupy the middle (or "core") of a sculpture and generally not seen.

It is less expensive than the drummed rope fibers which can be used to cover the core fiber. Batting felts easily and can be used to quickly establish basic shapes.

Loose fiber has many appearances depending upon the source of fiber.

Pictured are the locks a Romney sheep, on the left, and the locks of a Shetland sheep on the right.

SIZE – FIRMNESS - SHAPE

With drummed ropes of fiber, you can pull of a length of fiber that is, for example, 6" long.

You should be able to easily pull off another 6" section of roped fiber. While not absolutely exact, the two 6" sections of roped fiber are extremely similar in quantity.

You can split drummed rope fiber lengthwise into halves, quarters, or sixteenths.

As long as the initial length of drummed rope fiber was similar in length, any division of that length can be easily estimated and achieved as long as you are working with the same drummed rope fiber.

Ropes of fiber are not always of uniform thickness.

The mustard roped fiber in the photo on the right has a thicker rope than does the blue.

With experience, you will learn how to adjust for such differences with increasing ease. When measuring equal parts from different ropes you need to look for similarity in both length and density.

Batting comes in "sheets" and it is relatively simple to tear off a section that is 4" x 4" or 5" x 10" as needed.

As long as you are measuring from the same sheet of batting or batting made by the same manufacturer, such measurements are close enough for needle felting.

You could cut bat fiber with scissors, but tearing works well enough.

Loose fiber is perhaps the hardest to measure evenly. You can visually guess at equal quantities of fiber and, should your guess prove inaccurate, make corrections during the felting process by adding or removing fiber as needed. You are also less likely to need equal portions of loose fiber.

Needle felting affords you many opportunities to recognize problems, whether in the quantity of fiber or the placement of an elbow, and correct them as you are working.

Weezard Gnomes

SIZE – FIRMNESS - SHAPE

FIRMNESS:

To become very proficient with needle felting, you must learn to control the firmness of the fiber. There is not an ideal firmness that is suitable for all projects. How firm a piece should be depends on many factors, but most commonly is determined by the intended purpose of the piece, for example a pincushion need not be as firmly felted as a sculpture. The more firmly a piece is felted the more resilient it is to wear and tear. Needle felted toys that will endure a lot of play need to be well felted, but not necessarily very firmly felted. It seems a bit confusing, doesn't it?

Let's see if we can't make some sense of "firmness".

To demonstrate the various types of firmness, I created a triangular "log" out of white core fiber which I then covered with a blue surface fiber. I'm going to visually walk you through three stages of firmness: "medium firm", "firm" and "very firm".

SIZE – FIRMNESS - SHAPE

Needle Felting – to the Point

Here is a cross section cut from the "medium firm" log.

If I pinched it between my fingers it would give considerably. It is soft and spongy to the touch. When compressed it will spring back to its original shape, but repeated compression will eventually cause it to felt further. This could result in a loss in size and shape.

It is a reasonably strong structure that would require some effort to physically tear it apart.

For a pincushion this might be an ideal firmness.

This second cross section has been further reduced in size, increasing its overall firmness. It is still in the range of "medium firm", but is both smaller in size and denser than the previous example.

Reduction of size increases firmness.

Notice how more of the blue surface fiber can be seen within the white core fiber. As the triangular log is further reduced in size and increased in firmness, more and more of the blue fibers will be visible.

SIZE – FIRMNESS - SHAPE

Needle Felting – to the Point

A third cross section, after additional reduction of the log, reveals even more blue fiber mixed with the core fiber.

Now the triangle is beginning to become "firm". There is still "give", but much less than on the medium-firm triangles.

Repeated handling may result in additional felting, but with less change from the original piece than with the medium firm structures.

The more the log is reduced, the firmer it becomes. The firmer it becomes, the more entangled and felted the fibers are. The more entangled and felted the fibers are the more stable is the resulting structure.

At this stage (firm) there is still enough "give" to the overall structure to allow for a fair amount of manipulation.

"Give" is important!

SIZE – FIRMNESS - SHAPE

Needle Felting – to the Point

This fifth reduction of the log is "firm". The blue fiber is becoming ever more uniformly distributed in the white core fiber.

It takes a little more effort to insert the needles into a firm structure than it does to insert them into a medium firm structure.

The firmer an object becomes the more effort it will take to further increase its firmness. Elbow grease certainly will work, as will smaller gauge needles.

The sixth and final example from my triangular log is "very firm". It gives very little when I pinch it. The blue surface fiber is evenly distributed in the core fiber. It is dense and very solid.

Very firm structures are very stable. There is still a little bit of "give". With effort and smaller and smaller needles I could reduce it even further to the point where almost no further manipulation is possible.

SIZE – FIRMNESS - SHAPE

Firmness determines how durable a piece will be. The firmer the piece, the more durable it is. A piece that is very firmly felted is hard and dense which may not be the qualities you desire if you are making a child's toy. A piece that is medium firm will be softer to the touch and be more "cuddly", but may not withstand a lot of loving.

When you are needle-felting fiber, you are always looking for that balance of firmness which is appropriate for the expected life and purpose of what you are making.

If you were being very observant when viewing the triangular sections, you might have noted how the corners of the triangles became increasingly sharper the denser the triangles became.

The more firmly felted the fiber the more detail is possible, but that detail is defined and refined DURING the reduction of the fiber, NOT after it has been reduced.

When you are extremely accomplished as a needle felter, you might make a piece to which no further modifications are possible, but during the construction process you want your fiber to have some "give". Give allows you to manipulate the fiber, make corrections or simply sculpt it exactly how you want. You can learn to anticipate how much reduction is possible to achieve not only the look you desired, but the desired firmness as well.

It may take some time to develop such skill. In the meantime, it is worth knowing how to solve problems as they arise. In the process of sculpting fiber, you will work from less firm to more firm. The time to note what problems exist so that they may be solved is while the work is still in its less firm stage.

Fiber that is of medium firmness is very "plastic". A great amount of manipulation can be done before it becomes firm or very firm.

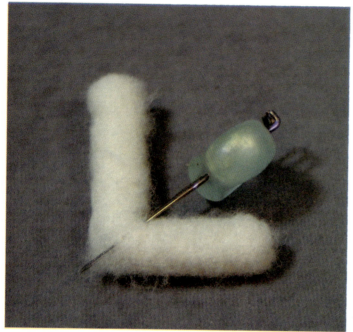

For example, you can bend and needle a medium firm log to form a right angle.

Such manipulation is excellent for forming elbows, heels or the corner of a frame.

Because some fibers originate in the vertical portion of this log and end in the horizontal portion, the bent piece is stronger than if two separate pieces had been joined.

Medium firm pieces can be bent into almost any shape you might need.

Medium firm structures are not strong and can just as easily be manipulated out of shape.

To lock in a shape that you begin forming with a medium firm piece, you have to increase the firmness with the addition of more fiber and/or a reduction of size.

SIZE – FIRMNESS - SHAPE

Needle Felting – to the Point

Some shapes are stronger than others. This circle is stronger than the squiggle in the previous photo, but it too is weak until the joint between the two ends is reinforced and equalized in firmness with additional fiber.

Once the joint has been reinforced and the firmness equalized, this circle is a stable form which can easily be manipulated because it is still medium firm.

Medium firm can be thought of as being twice the size of VERY firm.

SIZE – FIRMNESS - SHAPE

Needle Felting – to the Point

Details should be started when the fiber is still in a very "plastic" state such as medium firmness.

Here I have needled in a continuous line around the donut.

There is enough detail for you to see the line, but this piece as a whole is not stable. It is soft and spongy and could distort if handled repeatedly, could distort. The needled lines would remain, but the overall thickness of the piece could be reduced or distorted into an oval.

Further needling towards the center will reduce its size and increase its firmness.

If I wished for the size to remain the same while increasing the firmness, I would need to add more fiber.

The indentations are actually firmer than the areas in between, simply because I have needled them more.

I also needled this piece almost exclusively towards the center. The result is that not only does the whole piece become firmer and smaller in size, but also the hole in the middle becomes increasingly smaller.

If I had continually needled towards the outside as I sculpted, the hole in the middle would have become increasingly larger.

I could have made a ring to wear on my finger.

The piece is now "firm", although it could be further reduced to become "very firm".

It is now almost half the size of the original donut from which it was sculpted.

CORRECTING LENGTH:

Here I have three cylinders of similar size and firmness. They could be legs, or tree trunks, or something else completely. These are all medium firm, which means they will hold their shape, would not support weight well, and would give easily if pinched.

A medium firm object can be altered easily through a variety of different techniques.

Needling uniformly towards the middle will increase firmness and shorten the length of the piece.

Because the length is being reduced there will be less reduction of circumference.

Needle Felting – to the Point

After reducing evenly towards the center the middle piece is about an inch shorter in length and is denser and firmer than the other two pieces.

While shorter in length, it still appears to be about the same circumference as the other logs.

The top piece was made longer simply by rolling the piece between my palms. You can also lengthen a piece by grabbing the opposite ends and pulling.

Because this piece has been made longer, it is less firm than either of the other two pieces. It would be necessary to add more fiber to the top piece to have it match the firmness of either of the other two pieces.

In the previous photos, I altered the length of two of the three pieces. Both alterations changed not only the size of the pieces, but also their firmness. There are other methods for altering the length of an object without significantly changing the firmness.

CORRECTING LENGTH

Needle Felting – to the Point

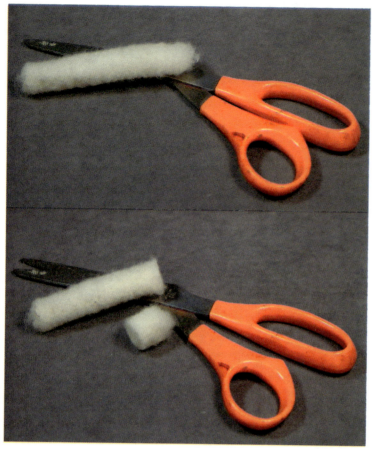

If you needed the piece to be shorter, but retain the same firmness as the original piece, you could either tear or cut off the excess length.

Tearing excess length will affect the firmness of the area from which it has been torn.

Cutting excess length will have little or no effect on the firmness of the area from which it is cut, but results in a very flat end.

Needle felters, as a rule, prefer feathered or non-defined ends which are easier to attach and disguise when joined with other pieces. Choosing the best solution depends on what you are making.

You could add length by adding more fiber to one end of your piece.

To demonstrate this, I have taken the bit I cut off in the previous photos and will add it back.

Note that I have feathered the fibers at the cut end of the longer of the two pieces. I have done this not only to help hide where I will join the pieces together, but also to help strengthen that join.

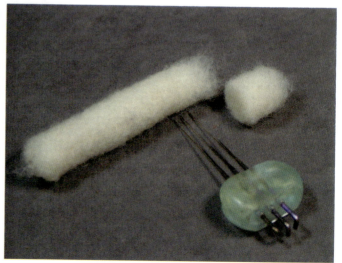

CORRECTING LENGTH

Needle Felting – to the Point

I've flipped the smaller piece around so that the cut end will be at the right and the rounded end is nested in the feathered fibers of the longer piece.

These can then be felted together and additional fiber can be added to match the firmness of the rest of the log, as well as strengthen the joining of these two pieces.

If you are going to do further manipulation to such a piece, lengthening it in this manner will work perfectly well. With further felting, more fibers will be shared between the two pieces and will truly make them one.

If you are not going to do significantly more felting it would be wiser to increase the length of the whole piece and add more fiber to the circumference to equalize the firmness.

Correcting length can be done by needling directionally to cause the object to become shorter or become longer, and by physically manipulating (pulling, squashing) the object itself. These methods will also alter the firmness of the object.

Adding or removing fiber can alter the length without significantly changing the firmness.

Which is better? It depends on what you are making. Whatever you make, you want there to be a consistency of firmness that is suited for the object's purpose, but if one part is just a little more or less firm than the rest it is not a significant difference. This is "GIVE" – that magically little "fudge factor" that allows you to make necessary alterations so that your finished piece is how you want it to be without sacrificing the integrity of the whole.

CORRECTING LENGTH

Needle Felting – to the Point

Felting needles are powerful tools for moving fiber around to where it is needed. You can always add fiber if necessary, but then you must disguise that the fiber was added. This isn't particularly difficult to do, but there are times when using a needles ability to move fiber from one place to another makes more sense.

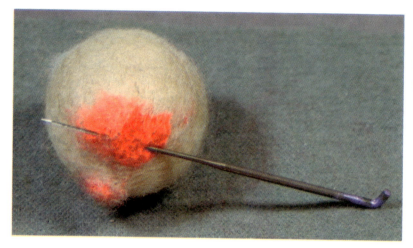

In the example on the left I have used bright red wool to show how needles can move fiber from one place to another.

It is possible to move it anywhere on the piece.

This is especially useful when sculpting. When sculpting a face, for example, a cheek or a chin may end up reducing more than expected.

You can use your needles to move fiber from an unimportant area or an area that will not be seen into the area where the additional fiber is needed.

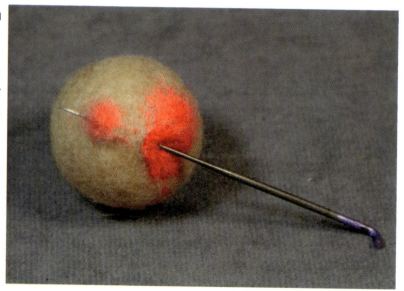

MOVING FIBER

Needle Felting – to the Point

You can add more fiber by creating a slit away from where the fiber is actually needed and then using your needles to move it into place.

Here I've carefully inserted a dark turquoise fiber into a deep slit that I made in the existing beige sphere.

The addition of fiber in this manner will increase the overall firmness of the sphere.

This new fiber can be completely stuffed inside the existing sphere. In my first book, I referred to this as "stuffing the tube", adding additional fiber to an existing form to increase its firmness.

Unless you felt deeply, fiber added in this manner is not actually felted, merely stuffed into a felted form.

The slit made to insert this fiber can be felted closed and completely obscured with the addition of some surface fiber. In this photo I have obscured half of the slit so that you can see how effective this method is for adding fiber and eliminating all traces of the addition.

In a larger piece, many such slits for stuffing the tube could be made and then hidden as needed.

Here the sphere has been "healed" leaving no trace as to where the slit and the fiber were added.

This can be a useful method for corrections when the addition of fiber on the surface of the object makes less sense.

MOVING FIBER

Needle Felting – to the Point

Learning great control of "Directional Needling" provides greater control of an object and firmness.

Here I have a core fiber log covered with blue and yellow "dress" fiber.

I will sometimes make experimental objects of this nature to practice directional needling and improve my control of the fiber shape and firmness.

Through careful reduction I created this extremely firm object in the photo.

The yellow area was not significantly reduced in length, but has taken on a tapered appearance with four flat sides.

The blue area was reduced in length but maintains the same diameter as the original log.

I also used my needles to transfer blue fiber down into the yellow area to demonstrate the great ability of needles to move fiber.

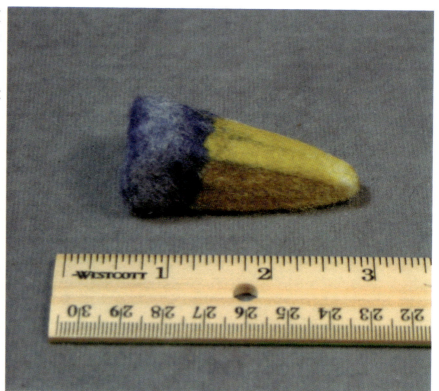

MOVING FIBER

RUNNING OUT OF A COLOR:

This may have happened to you already, and if not it most certainly will happen to you sooner or later. You're working on a project and discover that you do not have enough fiber in a particular color as you expected. What to do?

The sooner that you discover you have insufficient fiber of a particular color, the more options you have.

There are several possible solutions to this problem:

Buy more fiber in the needed color. This is a great solution if you can easily get the fiber or can wait for the fiber to arrive, but what if you can't wait?

You could change the color of fiber you intended to use to another of which you know you have sufficient quantities.

You could also extend the quantity of color you have by blending another color into the main color.

Sometimes you can match the color by blending two different colors together. The lower portion of this egg is covered in a solid color. I was able to closely match this color by blending blue and red together. It isn't an exact match, but very close.

The blended fiber has a bit of a "heather" look to it, with some areas being slightly redder and other areas being slightly bluer. I also blended a middle area which included some of the original solid color, making the transition from solid color to blended color more even.

The blended fiber could be used in areas that will not be seen, such as under hair or a beard if this color was being used for a garment.

You might be able to add a new element to your original idea which would eliminate some of the area that would have been covered with the original color.

By adding the draped cape at the back of this Gnome's outfit, I eliminated the need to use the maroon colored fiber in that area.

When running low on a color, figure out which areas must be seen, which areas could be hidden, and which areas could be replaced with another color altogether.

You could blend colors to completely blend out of the color you originally intended to use.

The egg on the left was transitioned from red to blue using three different blends. The 3 blended colors do appear as stripes, but if you were to make 5 or more blends and carefully feather over each area, you could make the transition appear seamless.

This is a very useful solution, but not applicable to every possible project.

Another solution is to use design to transition from one color to another.

The possible patterns that you can use to transition from one color to another are limitless.

I've created four examples here using just two colors, but you could use as many colors as you want.

If you are making an animal, you can give its coat a pattern. An orange cat could become a calico cat. A brown dog could have white spots.

There are many creative solutions to use when running out of a particular color!

Needle Felting – to the Point

In my first book I used many projects to demonstrate concepts and techniques in needle felting fiber, but I did not include step-by-step instructions for making them although there was enough information, between the photos and text, to figure out how to make those projects.

In this book I am including a number of projects which will include step-by-step instruction, but the emphasis is not merely on making these projects but also on learning how to problem solve.

All of the included projects are beginner to intermediate level. You should know how to make basic forms such as spheres, eggs, etc. You should know how to flat felt. You should understand the basic forms of needling: deep needling, needle in place, surface felting etc. Making these projects should help you to acquire these skills if you do not already have them. It is my hope that you will also learn how to solve problems as they arise and to learn, most importantly, that needle felting with fiber is very forgiving. Try and don't be afraid of the failure! Success is just a few pokes away!

Projects included in this book are:
    Winged Mouse
    Frog
    Squirrel
    Gnome
    Ferret
    Fairy
    Woodland Diorama

Useful tools for needle felting include:
    Scissors
    Wire cutters and wire
    2 wire dog brushes for blending fiber
    Doll needles
    Thread and needles
    Long straight pins
    Pliers
    Sweater shaver
    Glue

Needle Felting – to the Point

WINGED MOUSE – Materials needed:

Core Fiber
Merino fiber:
    Dark and Medium Brown
    Contrasting color for wings
Glass Black Beads
Needle and thread
Feathers (optional)
Small leaf shaped cookie cutter (optional)

This cute little mouse is a simple project. He isn't overly detailed, but has a lot of charm.

Take a piece of Core Fiber that is about 3" x 5" in size.

I always like to use core fiber as my foundation in needle felting because it not only felts quickly, but also because it provides strength which is not easily achieved using pure Merino fiber. Core fiber comes as batting which makes it easy to establish basic foundation shapes.

Roll the core fiber into a log and felt it sufficiently to hold it together.

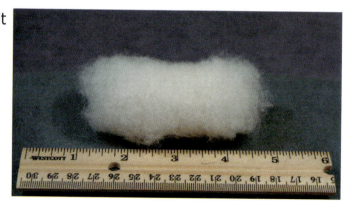

Needle Felting – to the Point

Shape your core fiber log into the rough shape of a sitting mouse.

The overall firmness of the foundation will increase.

The head area should be slightly firmer than the body area.

The shape does not need to be perfect.

Blend equal quantities of your dark and medium brown fibers.

It is alright to cut the fiber into 1" to 1.5" lengths with scissors for the purpose of blending the two colors.

The color choice is yours - you could choose to make a grey mouse, or a lighter colored brown mouse or even a purple mouse.

You could choose to make a solid color mouse.

Cover the foundation with the blended fiber. Fiber used to cover a foundation is "dress" fiber.

The addition of the blended fiber will further increase the firmness of the mouse and allow you to begin refining its shape.

At this stage you need only be concerned with getting even coverage of the blended fiber.

WINGED MOUSE

Once the foundation is completely covered, surface felt the "dress" fiber well to the foundation core fiber.

Surface felting the dress fiber will not only smooth the surface and increase the firmness of the overall piece, but also improve your ability to refine and sculpt it.

I've used small quantities of the blended fiber to make paws.

Take a small quantity of the blended color and blend additional medium brown into it to create a lighter brown.

Using a very small quantity, roll it in the palm of one hand with the finger tips of the other hand to form a tiny sphere. This will become the nose.

This sphere should be a bit larger than you want the finished nose to be.

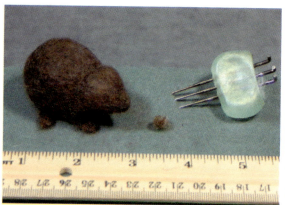

Attach the sphere to the head using a fine felting needle.

You can see in this photo that the nose looks terribly large for a mouse. In fact at this stage that long nose makes it look a lot more like a mole than a mouse.

Reduce the size of the nose.

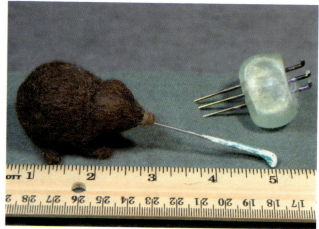

Use thread and a needle to attach two black beads for eyes.

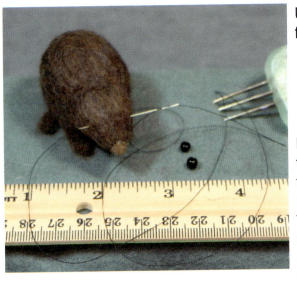

Pass the needle through the head, but do not pull the knot against the head. Pick up a bead and pass the needle back through the head. Next pass the needle between the threads near the knot.
This will prevent the knot from being pulled through the head when you pull the thread tight. Pick up the other bead and pass the needle back through the head.

Use your thumb and finger to press the glass bead eyes into the head while using your other hand to pull the thread taught.

Secure the thread prior to cutting. I like to pass my needle and thread back and forth through the head several times instead of making a knot. I call this "burying the thread" and find that it is just as secure as making another knot.

Adding the eyes created some thinness of fiber over the cheek area.

Tearing off some short fibers of the blended fiber and surface felting them over the thin area will resolve that problem.

The process of sculpting or adding eyes creates tension on the fiber in the nearby areas. This can result, as it did here, in the dress fiber becoming thin and exposing the core fiber below. Simply add a small quantity of the dress fiber to resolve the problem and surface felt it into place.

Needle Felting – to the Point

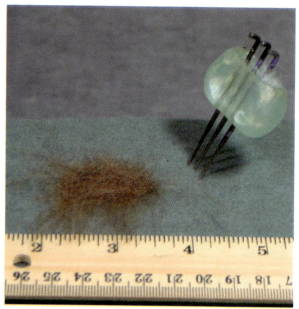

To make the ears you will need to flat felt two semi-circles.

Mice ears are lighter in color than their body so use the lighter blend of brown you created for making the nose.

Lay thin layers of fiber slightly larger than the size of the ear you wish to create on your work surface. Tack the fibers together and use your needles to outline a half circle.

Gently fold the fibers outside the half circle towards the middle, and then flat felt well from both sides. The bottom edge remains unfelted.

Make a matching ear and then pin both into place on your mouse.

Pinning ears into place gives you the chance to check their position, and even to pose them prior to felting into place. I sometimes end up using as many as three pins per ear to position them exactly as I want.

It is easier to use pins to position the ears correctly than to just lightly felt them into place, only to have to remove the ears to reposition them later.

WINGED MOUSE

Needle Felting – to the Point

I've placed my mouse's ears in a very simple position, but you may wish to experiment with other positions.

You could make the ears lay back against the body, more towards the head or perhaps to the side.

Such small variations in position can completely alter the look of your mouse providing your own unique characterization.

When you are satisfied with their position, felt the ears firmly into the head.

There are many different ways to make a tail. For this mouse I used a twist and felt process using the lighter color brown blend.

From your mass of fiber, gently pull to form a tip. Anchor that tip to your work surface with a felting needle and begin to gently twist and pull the fiber. As you pull and twist, use another needle to felt the twisted fiber.

As you continue to twist and felt the fiber for the tail, you will need to allow more fiber in order to gradually increase the diameter.

If an area has too little fiber, use your needles to drag more into that area.

Make the tail as long as you wish and then gently pull away any excess blended fiber. Felt your tail well. By controlling the direction of your needles you can correct any unwanted variances of thickness.

WINGED MOUSE

When your tail is well felted, roll it lightly between your palms.

This process will smooth the surface.

If it was not quite as long as you wished, applying more pressure as you roll the tail between your palms will lengthen it.

It will also reduce the diameter of the tail.

Attach the tail by deep felting the loose fiber at the base into the mouse body.

Oops! I accidentally felted my mouse's tail off center a problem I might have avoided had I pinned it into place and carefully checked its position before I felted it into place.

This is easily corrected.

Gently pull the tail away from the body. This will reveal the fibers from the tail that were deep felted into the body.

Use a felting needle to drag those fibers back out of the body.

My tail wasn't seriously off center, so I only need to free half of the deep felted tail fibers and then rotate to position it correctly.

Needle Felting – to the Point

Once properly positioned, deep felt the fibers into the body.

To add greater security to the join between body and tail, you should also felt from the underside of the body into the center of the tail. Avoid felting to the outside of the tail.

To do this you may need to hold the tail in place to resist the pressure of the needle so be careful not to poke yourself!

I knew I wanted wings for this little mouse, but I wasn't quite sure how they should be made.

My first idea was to use some feathers. I cut some feathers to a size about a .5" larger than seen in this photo and trimmed .5" of the shaft to insert into the body.

I used a large needle to create a hole into which I could insert the trimmed shafts.

I wasn't really happy with this look, so I decided to try something else.

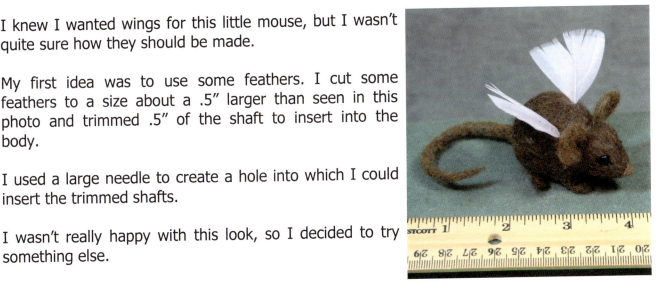

Using a small leaf shaped cookie cutter as a flat felting mold, I flat felted two purple wings.

I then trimmed a fluffier section of the feathers I used in the previous photo and, with the use of a small quantity of purple fiber, felted the fluffy feathers to the back of the purple wings.

I liked these wings much better, but there are so many possibilities! Experiment and find your own perfect solution!

Needle Felting – to the Point

Something had been bothering me about my mouse, eventually I realized that the paws were the wrong color.

Mouse paws should be the same color as the ears and tail.

Using small quantities of the lighter brown blended fiber, I made new paws.

Now how to make the correction?

Snip off the old dark paws and use a felting needle to drag fibers out from the cut edge.

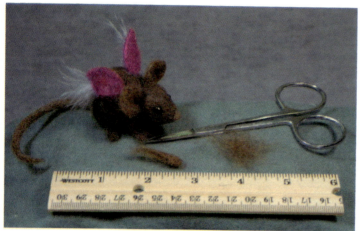

Deep felt the new lighter colored paw into place and use the feathered fibers from the cut to soften the transition between body and paws. Repeat the process until all four paws are the lighter brown.

This process of cutting off a part that doesn't work, feathering the edges of the cut and adding a new part that does work can be used for more than just correcting the color of mice paws.

WINGED MOUSE

He does look a lot better with the lighter colored paws!

It wasn't at all a difficult correction to make.

On the mouse, the head is a little firmer than the body. The difference is not excessive.

To create the nice curve in the tail, I overlapped the tip of the tail near the base, forming a circle. I then pinned it in that position overnight. The curve could be further secured by lightly felting the tail in the curved position.

What starts out as just loose fiber can, with time and effort, be shaped as desired.

Sculpting or the addition of eyes puts pressure on the fiber that can result in thin areas where the core fiber is revealed. The solution is to add a layer of fiber to cover the thin area and then felt it into the whole.

Use straight pins to position parts onto your sculpture. Doing so gives you the opportunity to reposition the parts as needed and try different poses.

Major corrections can be made by cutting off the incorrect part, feathering the cut edge and adding the new part. Twice in my years of making needle felted sculptures I have cut off the heads of creatures and replaced them.

Needle Felting – to the Point

FROG – Materials needed:
  Core Fiber
  Merino "dress fiber"   I used a blend of blue & green
  Eyes (these are plastic fishing lure eyes)

The frog begins in much the same manner as did the mouse.

Roll core fiber (3"x5") into a log. Felt to secure the log and then sculpt into a roughly frog shaped body.

The frog's head is a bit flatter than that of the mouse and the back end is more "V" shaped than the rounded hindquarters of the mouse.

Many different creatures could be made starting with this basic shape.

Cover the core fiber foundation with "dress" fiber and surface felt well into the foundation.

FROG

Needle Felting – to the Point

Use an Exacto knife to cut slits to insert the eyes.

Plastic fishing lure eyes such as these are transparent. To make the color visible, paint the backs of the irises white and allow to dry.

Use a small quantity of glue on the stem to secure in place.

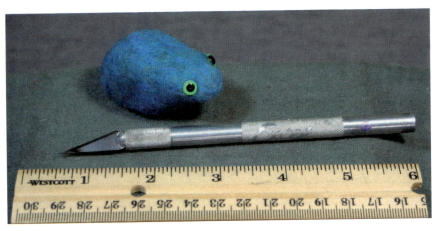

Flat felt two narrow sections of fiber long enough to encircle each eye.

Attach the flat felted piece around the eye as shown. The eye will be hardly visible during this stage.

FROG

Needle Felting – to the Point

Use your needles to gently reduce the eye "cuff". You need to needle the outside edge next to the eye, and then reduce the fiber.

This method of flat felting narrow strips can also be used to create eyelids on figures, but in this case we're just building up the bulge that naturally surrounds a frog's eye.

When completed, the added flat felted fiber should look more like the photo on the left.

You can add a line of darker fiber around the eye itself to increase the contrast between eye and body color.

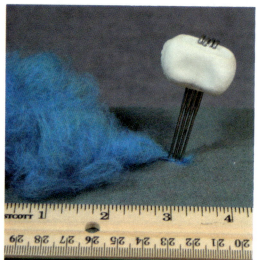

Fingers for the feet are made by twisting and felting the fiber in the same manner as the mouse's tail was made, but on a much smaller scale.

This is an extremely useful technique!

If your twisted fiber is too thick you can gently pull on the loose fibers or use your needles to directionally force fibers out of the twist.

If your twist is too thin, you can use your needles to drag fibers into the twist and felt again.

FROG

Needle Felting – to the Point

A total of twelve digits are needed for the frog's feet. After twist felting the digits, roll the felted section between palm and finger to smooth the surface.

The tips of the toes are made from small spheres. These spheres should be firmer than the one used for the mouse nose.

To attach the spheres to the tips of the digits, felt the tip fiber through the spheres and then back into the digit.

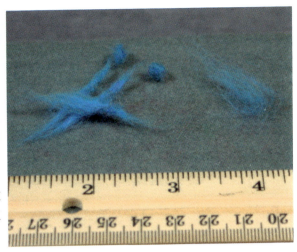

Notice the difference between the front and back feet of the frog.

Lay your sphere tipped digits out in these patterns and use a small quantity of fiber to felt them together.

Do remember that there are right and left front feet. One foot will have the shorter digit on the inside left and the other on the inside right. If you forget to make a right and a left, you can turn one of your front feet over.

When all digits have been felted into feet, condense the loose fiber nearest the foot into a wrist/ankle as seen in the foot on the left of this photo.

You will still need loose fiber at the end of the wrists/ankle for joining to the legs.

If necessary, you can add more fiber to create the wrists/ankles.

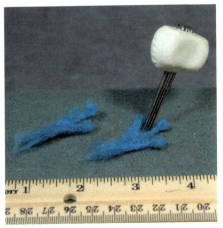

FROG

Attach loose fiber to the wrist and using the twist and felt method create two front arms.

These need to be long enough to reach from the shoulder to the ground and include an elbow bend as seen in this photo.

Attach the front legs as seen in the photo on the right.

As you can also see, the top of that arm looks rather bad. I will show you two ways to correct that problem, but first we'll get the rest of the legs added.

To make the rear legs, attach loose fiber to the back foot. There needs to be enough fiber to form the reverse "V" shown in the photo by orange lines. The upper arm of this "V" is much thicker than the lower.

I chose to twist felt the lower section, create the heel bend and then felt the upper portion directly onto the body.

FROG

Needle Felting – to the Point

With all four legs attached, the frog looks like this.

We know that the join at the shoulder is rather ugly and obvious, but it also appears that the nose is a bit short on this guy as well.

He certainly doesn't look bad, but we will lengthen his nose, before we're done, to demonstrate how such problems can easily be solved with the careful addition of more fiber.

One method to obscure where the top of the arm was joined to the body just behind the eye is to add a small quantity of fiber to cover up the obvious join. The additional fiber is then surface felted into the body.

Another method to correct such problems is to use your needles to drag fibers out of the top of the arm and felt those into the body.

Both of these methods work perfectly well.

The first may be more useful if you also need/want to add more fiber to the arm itself.

FROG

Needle Felting – to the Point

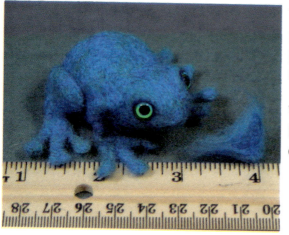

To lengthen the nose, I used loose fiber felted into a pyramid shape with loose fibers at the edges. This pyramid is medium firm at best since I want to be able to attach it properly to the existing nose.

When adding fiber in this manner, the form should be larger than you wish the end result to be, and only roughly shaped.

The feathered edges of the new nose are attached and felted into the body of the frog. At this stage the new nose will appear to be too long; this is easily corrected by gently felting the addition into the old nose.

Refine its shape as you reduce the fiber until the addition is exactly as you wish it to be.

Small quantities of fiber can be used to obscure bad joins.

Fiber can be dragged out of one piece and then felted to also obscure a bad join.

Fiber can be added to transform and/or correct the shape of an existing piece.

Needle Felting – to the Point

SQUIRREL – Materials needed:

Core Fiber
Merino Fiber – light and dark brown
Black glass beads for eyes
Needle and thread

Make a small, firm sphere of core fiber.

Cover the sphere with "dress" fiber and create a medium firm cone of fiber to be added to the sphere.

I use this method of adding a medium firm cone to a firmer sphere when I intend to sculpt the cone area.

When the sphere and cone are joined together they form a nice egg is of variable firmness. The sphere portion will not be sculpted and, being firmer than the cone area, will remain stable in shape and size.

The cone, being medium firm, allows for greater manipulation, allowing you to more easily sculpt the features of the muzzle.

SQUIRREL

Needle Felting – to the Point

Sculpting the face begins with creating a "V" for the nose.

Change the "V" to a "Y" to create the separation between the two halves of the muzzle.

Change the "Y" to an "X" and you've created a mouth.

Use a small amount of blended dark and medium brown fiber to form a small pyramid. This pyramid will be transformed into the nose.

Attach the small pyramid of darker fiber to the head. Reduce and shape it into a nose.

Add darker fiber into the lines defining the muzzle and mouth.

Use needle and thread to attach the glass beads for eyes.

When returning the needle to the knot side, remember to insert the needle through the two threads near the knot.

Add the second bead and pass the needle to the other side of the head. Pull the thread taught to cause the eyes to be indented. Secure the thread.

SQUIRREL

Needle Felting – to the Point

Here you see the eyes are slightly recessed into the head.

If you are happy with this look, you could skip the next step, the addition of eyelids.

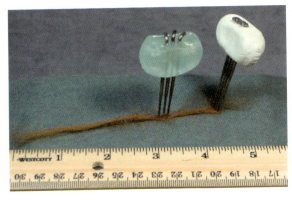

Take a small quantity (about 4" in length) of your drum carded fiber. Secure one end to your work surface with felting needles.

Twist and felt the length of fiber.

Lift the fibers and twist and felt again until you have formed a fuzzy "yarn".

The fuzzy texture of the "yarn" created allows it to be felted nicely around the eye.

I started at the inner corner of the eye, felting and securing the eyelid into place. When the whole eye is encircled, trim the excess "yarn" at a slight angle. Felt the end into the head.

The eyelid is still a bit visible in this photo. This isn't a bad look, but to completely obscure where the eyelid was added, use your needles to drag out a few fibers from the eyelid and felt them to the head.

This is the same feathering of the fibers that was done on the left arm of the toad.

SQUIRREL

Needle Felting – to the Point

Ears are made by laying out a thin layer of fiber as wide, top to bottom, as the height of the ears.

A second thin layer of fiber is laid perpendicular to the first layer as seen in the photo.

Tack the layers together lightly with your needles.

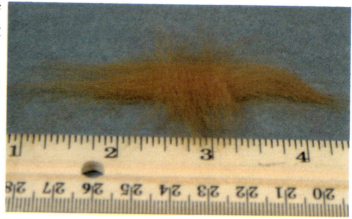

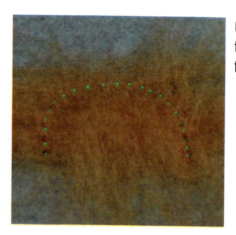

Use your needles to outline the basic shape for the ear. Fold the excess fiber in towards the middle and flat felt the ear from both sides.

The fibers at the bottom of the ear (where it will attach to the head), should remain unfelted.

Make two matching ears.

Pin the ears to the head. When you are satisfied with their position, felt them firmly to the head.

SQUIRREL

To make the body, tear off some core fiber roughly 3.5" x 5" in size. Roll the core fiber into a log and felt until secure.

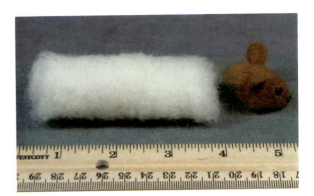

Roughly shape the log for the squirrel body.

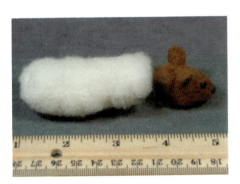

My squirrel is meant to be climbing a tree so his body is rather flat and his head will be lifted slightly.

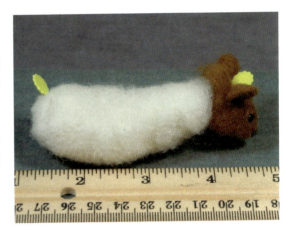

Use core fiber to create arms and legs.

I used one piece of core fiber to create both arms. The core fiber is very thin where it will attach to the body, but the arms have sufficient fiber to provide a good foundation.

I made two separate back legs.

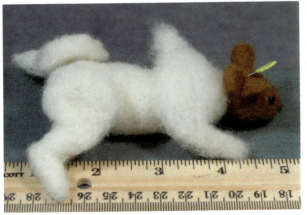

SQUIRREL

Needle Felting – to the Point

Attach the arms and legs to the body.

There is still enough "give" in the core fiber body that you can play around with the precise pose of your squirrel.

I decided to have my squirrel have its left rear leg bent, with the right rear leg stretched out, as seen in the photo.

Attach the head securely to the body and add "dress" fiber as needed.

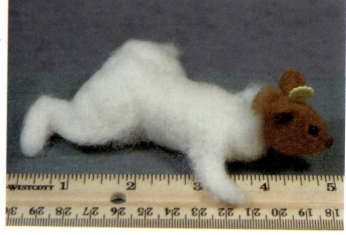

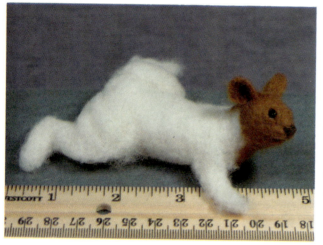

I adjusted the head and neck on my squirrel to make it appear as though he is looking around.

At this stage, it is still possible to turn the head to look left or right, higher or lower.

You will still be able to make some modifications to pose as the "dress" fiber is added, but you will need to establish a clear idea of that pose now.

Add the "dress" fiber.

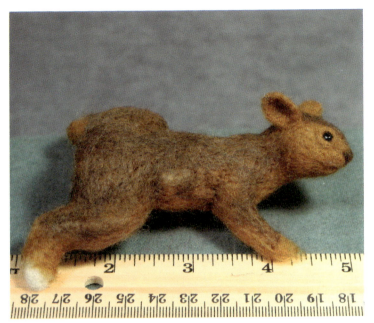

The underside of the squirrel is covered with the lighter brown fiber.

The back of the squirrel and part of the head is covered with a blend of the two browns.

In this photo you can see a few areas that have not been covered uniformly with the "dress" fiber.

Small additions of "dress" fiber will fix this problem.

There are still more thin areas that will need some additional dress fiber to correct. His shape is still a bit wonky and his paws look terrible.

I find that it is easier to refine the shape after the dress fiber has been applied.

It is easier to see the proportions and relationship between limbs and body when the sculpture is its final color.

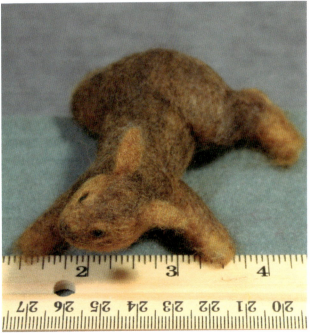

Make a core fiber foundation for the tail. The tail is about as long as the body of the squirrel.

If you prefer, you could make a tail foundation by twist felting blended brown fiber in the same manner as the tail for the mouse was made. If you do twist felt the foundation, it does not need to be particularly firm.

Tear off short lengths of your blended fiber and felt one end of the short fibers into the tail foundation.

Work from the tip of the tail to the base.

Rotate the tail so that you are adding fluffy fibers to all sides of the tail foundation.

Gently pull away any loose fluffy fiber that didn't get felted into the foundation.

Attach the tail firmly to the body.

Cover any thinness in the dress fiber.

That's not a bad squirrel, but with some minor changes he can be made much better.

Let's improve those paws!

Needle Felting – to the Point

Twist felt small digits from the lighter brown fiber.

Felt the digits into paws just as we did for the frog.

Attach the paws to the legs, overlapping the old rounded paws.

If the addition of the new paws makes the arms or feet seem too long, you can shorten their length by needling towards the elbows and/or heels.

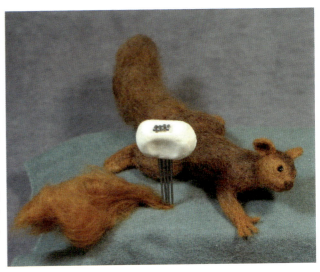

There he is – a nice little squirrel ready to climb a tree stump.

Many basic changes to the pose can be made while working with the core fiber foundation.

Refinements to the pose and corrections to the proportions can be made right up to the moment you are ready to call it "done".

The head of this squirrel is "very firm". The rest of the body is only "firm". There is still enough "give" in this sculpture to change the pose if desired. For example, the chest, neck and head could be lifted by bending the upper body from the waist and the new position locked into place by cross needling and deep needling at the bend.

This sculpture is very stable as it is, but there is sufficient "give" to allow for whatever artistic changes you might wish to make.

Needle Felting – to the Point

GNOME – Materials needed:

Core Fiber
Merino in flesh, pink (for cheeks and lip), mustard, red and blue
Shetland or similar specialty fiber for beard and Hair.
Norwegian C1 batting in brown for boots
Black seed beads
Needle and thread
Two tiny rusted jingle bells (optional)

You can choose to make a Gnome in whatever colors you prefer. Most of the Shetland fiber I have handled comes in white, off-white, grey, brown or black. It is possible to dye such fibers if you want the hair and beard to be a different color. Wool is easy to dye with food coloring.

> **Dyeing Wool:** Soak the wool to be dyed in a solution of very warm $4/5^{th}$ water and $1/5^{th}$ vinegar for about 30 minutes. The water/vinegar solution should cover the wool fiber. Add food coloring and distribute it evenly through the water/vinegar solution while avoiding agitating the wool. Place container in microwave and heat on high for 2 minutes. Check the container/wool. You want the solution to almost boil, so re-heat for 1-2 minute intervals as needed. As the wool absorbs the color, the water/vinegar solution will appear clearer i.e. less colored than when you originally added the food coloring. Rinse the wool in very warm water until the water runs clear. Dry on a cookie rack or similar well ventilated surface. Never agitate the wool fibers! If you do, you will cause them to felt!

Make a firm egg shape from core fiber.

I always start my creatures by making the head. I find it is easier to match the body to the head than the other way around.

If I were doing a more detailed humanoid figure, I would actually start with a skull shaped foundation.

For this project an, egg shape works perfectly well.

GNOME

Needle Felting – to the Point

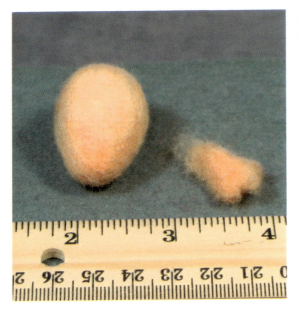

Cover the egg foundation with flesh colored "dress" fiber. Use carded fiber to create a relatively large nose.

When forming the nose, there should be more fiber in the tip than in the sides.

I like to attach the top of the nose first and then the tip.

Once tacked in place, begin to reduce and refine the shape of the nose, which will reduce in size and increase in firmness.

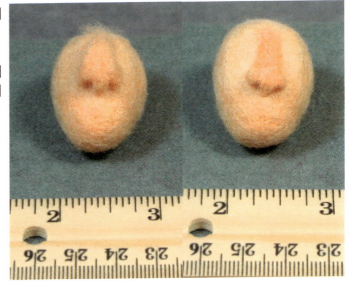

Needle Felting – to the Point

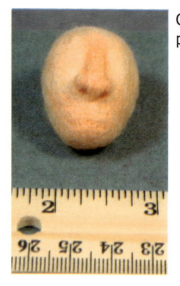

Continue to reduce and refine the shape of the nose until you are pleased with its appearance.

This is a fairly classic "Roman" nose, but you can create any shape you wish.

You may also note that there isn't much of a chin and the dome of the head is a bit small if you were planning to create a detailed sculpture of a head.

For this gnome, this shape works very well.

Blend small quantities of the flesh and pink colors to make a new color suitable for the lip and the blush on the cheeks.

Roll up a small quantity of the blush to form a lower lip and felt it into place. There is no need to make an upper lip since it will be hidden by the moustache.

Add blush to the cheeks. If you wanted to build up round, rosy cheeks, this is the perfect time to do so.

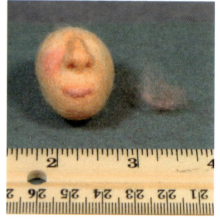

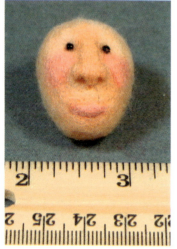

Add two seed beads for eyes. These eyes are attached and secured in the same way as on the mouse and the squirrel, except that the needle is inserted from the middle back of the head to the front.

There are many ways to alter the look of your gnome simply by altering the way you attach the eyes.

You can make them appear more deep-set by applying greater tension to the thread and indenting them deeper into the head. You can attach them so that your gnome is looking to the left or to the right. You could make your gnome look cross-eyed. You could add small quantities of shadow above the eyes.

GNOME

If you want to make ears for your gnome, you have a variety of options. I made tiny, pointed years by carefully flat felting small, narrow triangles.

You could make rounded ears if you prefer. Whatever shaped ears you make, keep in mind that the addition of hair will, to some degree, hide the ears.

It is better to make the ears a little larger than you might think they need to be.

If they end up being too large when the hair is applied, you can either fluff out the hair or felt the ears more deeply into the head.

Create a body for your gnome with core fiber. This is actually more like a tunic that would reveal only the boots below. A neck will be added later in the process.

My little gnome is fairly normal in size and shape, but you may wish to make your gnome thinner or fatter.

You can decide to give your gnome a plump tummy.

You might decide to give him a large barrel chest.

You could either make such changes to the basic shape now or wait until the dress fiber has been applied.

Needle Felting – to the Point

Before applying dress fiber to the torso, let's make the boots.

I used Norwegian C1 batting to make the boots. The texture of Norwegian C1 is very similar to Corriedale and coarser than Merino.

It felts quickly and provides a nice strength to the shape.

The rougher texture of this fiber gave the boots a rather "lived in" appearance. I can just see a gnome slogging around in such boots!

My gnomes have large feet! This is the evolutionary result of thousands upon thousands of years of playing acorn soccer.

Really!

Seriously, my gnomes have large feet because it is far easier to get them to stand properly when they have large feet.

It is perfectly possible to make smaller feet and have them stand quite nicely, but it takes a bit more effort to perfect the balance to make smaller feet work.

Large feet are cute and confuse predators into searching for taller prey.

Another explanation is: the boots are large and the feet are small which provides extra insulation for tiny gnome toes against the bitter cold of winter.

GNOME

Cover the torso/tunic with "dress" fiber.

My gnome will have a decorative belt and matching decoration on his cuffs, but you can decorate your gnome's clothes in any way you desire.

Use a small quantity of carded, flesh colored fiber to make small fists.

It is possible to make small hands using the twist and felt process to make fingers, arranging the fingers and using a small addition of fiber to felt the hand together and create the palm.

Fists are easier and look fine.

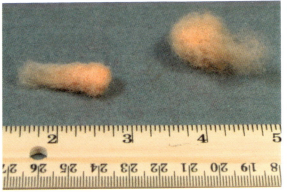

On such a small figure as our gnome, it is easiest to make the arms by making flexible sleeves.

Lay out a thin layer of fiber about an inch wide from top to bottom. Lay a thin layer of fiber perpendicular to the first layer as seen.

Tack the fibers together.

GNOME

Needle Felting – to the Point

Fold the long fibers in half and flat felt well at the cuff/fold. Remember to flat felt the cuff well from both sides.

Do not felt the rest of the loose fiber.

Check to see that the sleeve you have made will fit around the wrist of the fists you made in a previous step.

Any embellishments that you intend to add to the sleeve should be added prior to attaching the sleeve to the fist.

Here I have attached red and blue trim that will match the belt to be put on the gnome.

Felt the trim into the cuff securely. Only felt from the topside to avoid felting yellow fiber through the trim.

Position the sleeve around the fist and attach by felting through the cuff into the wrist.

Do not felt completely through the whole wrist or you may have flesh colored fiber show through on your cuff.

Fold excess fiber from the top of the sleeve back towards the cuff on the inside of the sleeve. Use your needles to condense and shape the fold into a nice rounded edge.

By not felting the fiber between shoulder and cuff, you will be able to pose the sleeve/arm more easily once it is attached to the gnome body.

Attach sleeves at the shoulders.

GNOME

Needle Felting – to the Point

Position your gnome's arms and felt at the cuff into the body.

I find that it is helpful to use a needle held against the middle of the unfelted section of the sleeve to help form the elbow.

Once the arm/sleeve is positioned as you like it, you can lightly felt the sleeve to reduce excessive puffiness.

You could try pinning your arms into different positions before finally felting into place.

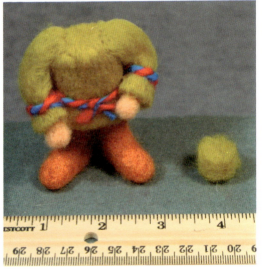

Make a neck for your gnome out of fiber matching his tunic. The neck is just a small fat log and should be medium firm.

The neck, in all probability, will not be seen. Once the hair and beard are attached, the neck isn't visible depending on how the hair and beard are arranged.

The neck should be "medium firm" to allow for better positioning of the head.

Attach the neck to the top of the torso by deep needling through the neck into the torso.

GNOME

Needle Felting – to the Point

Pin the head to the neck.

If you want your gnome looking to the left or to the right or looking up or down, now is the time to use pins to try different poses. Felt the head securely to the neck and body.

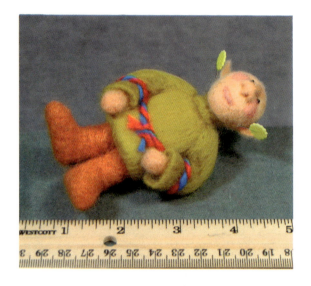

Once the head is securely attached, you can use the specialty fiber to create hair and beard.

I like to arrange the beard and the hair for the back of the head on my work surface prior to attaching to the head.

Don't forget to make eyebrows!

Needle Felting – to the Point

To make the hat, lay out a thin layer of fiber longer than the circumference needed and about an inch wide.

Lay a second thin layer of fiber perpendicular to the first. This second layer should extend well beyond the horizontal fibers.

Tack the layers together lightly and needle a straight line down the horizontal center.

This line is where the fibers will be folded back upon themselves to prepare for some really good flat felting.

Fold the fibers and flat felt well from both sides.

We're preparing to make a simple pillbox hat. The long vertical fibers will be used to create the top of the hat.

Overlap the ends to form a circle. You can trim any excess fiber if needed. Felt the overlapped edges together.

Fold the long fibers into the middle and felt to form the top of the hat and felt.

Add fiber if any portion of the top is too thin.

Felt well.

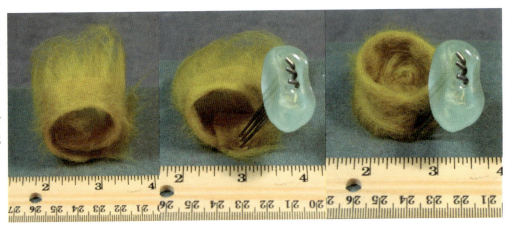

GNOME

Needle Felting – to the Point

Attach the hat to the gnome head and add whatever other finishing touches you like and you're done!

Weezard Gnomes

Needle Felting – to the Point

FERRET – Materials needed:
- Core Fiber
- Merino in white, brown and pink
- Glass beads for eyes
- Needle and thread

I used two browns (medium and dark) for my ferret. Ferrets come in different colors, so you may choose what colors you prefer.

Create a firm egg shape from core fiber. There is some sculpting to be done to the head, but none so extensive as to require creating an egg of variable firmness.

Cover the egg with a blend of mostly white and a little brown.

Sculpt the face as was done for the squirrel. There is not much space between the bottom of the nose and the mouth on a ferret.

FERRET

Needle Felting – to the Point

Blend a small amount of pink and white fiber for the nose. Form a "T" shape, which will assist in sculpting nostrils.

Flatten the area between nose and where the eyes will be set.

Ferrets have a rather triangular shaped head from the nose to slightly behind the eyes.

Attach and sculpt the nose.

Add darker fiber inside each nostril if you wish.

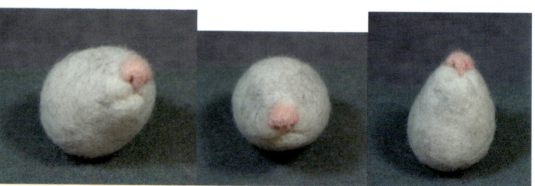

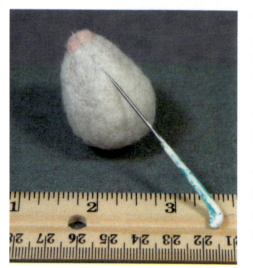

To soften the transition from head to nose, use a fine needle to move the white blend fiber from the head into the edge of the nose. The needle should remain very close to the surface when sharing fibers in this manner.

You could also do this in reverse, moving some of the blended nose fiber into the head

You could also try adding small quantities of fiber to soften the transition between the pink nose and white head, but sharing the fiber is easier, increases the join between head and nose, and gives you greater control.

FERRET

One of my muzzle areas was less plump than the other.

To correct this problem, I used needles to move fiber from further back on the head into the muzzle.

This same technique could be used to add more fiber/plumpness to the chin.

You could also use this technique to move too much fiber out of an area simply by reversing the direction of your needles.

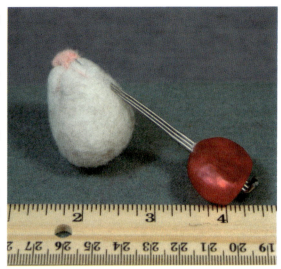

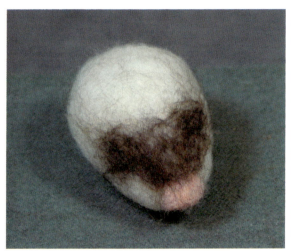

Add short lengths of the darker fiber to create a mask on the ferret head.

Note that this dark mask does not cover the cheek areas at the side of the nose.

Ferret markings are fairly uniform and symmetrical, but they are not all identical to the pattern I have laid out here.

Examine photos of ferrets for other facial marking options.

The eyes are attached by passing the needle from the middle back of the head to the eye socket.

Ferrets are predators with sharp stereoscopic vision. Their eyes need to face forward.

Pull the thread taught to indent the eye beads into the head.

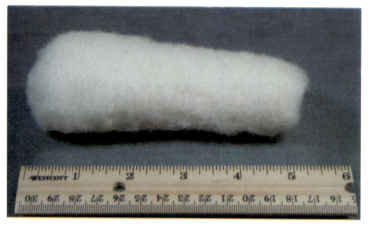

Ferret bodies are rather like torpedoes: long and narrow.

This suits their lifestyle which includes living in underground burrows.

Using core fiber, create a log about 5" in length and slightly thicker at the tail end.

Pin the ferret head to the narrower end of the body log.

Ferret necks are almost as thick as their upper body.

There is an increase in body thickness where the forelegs are joined, and we'll increase that thickness when those legs are added.

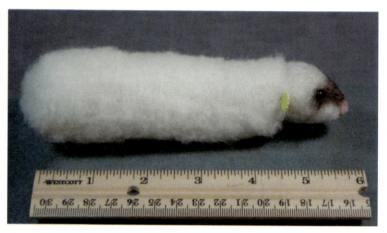

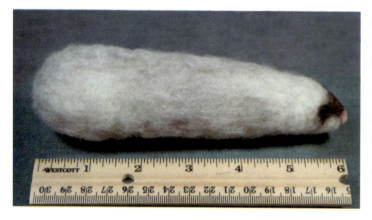

Cover the body with a slightly darker blend of white and brown than was used to cover the head.

Truthfully, I'm not quite certain that body is long enough, but that is a bit difficult to determine in this current pose.

We're going to forge ahead.

Needle Felting – to the Point

Create a bend for the neck at the back of the head.

Needle to secure the new shape of head and neck.

Now I can see that the body is definitely not looking long enough. The next step should tell us more.

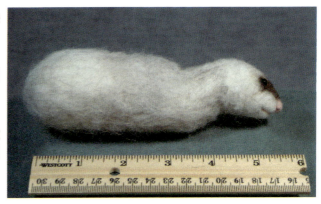

Manipulate the body log into a "S" shape and needle to secure.

You should not be changing the overall length of the body. You're shifting fiber down at the breastbone and up at the tummy.

The body appears longer in this "S" shape.

Create some flat felted ears for the ferret.

We've made such ears for both the mouse and the squirrel so I haven't included detailed photos.

It is the same process: lay out a thin layer of fiber horizontally and then place a thin second layer perpendicular on top. Tack the two layers together and needle the basic semicircle shape desired for the ear. Fold in the excess fiber and then flat felting well from both sides.

For the ferret ears, I made an additional set of thin pink ears which are slightly smaller in size. Lightly felt the pink ears to the white ears. Pin and felt into place.

Needle Felting – to the Point

Use core fiber to create two front legs.

Take the core fiber and roll it into a log to begin shaping the leg foundation. Bend one end to form a paw stub.

Do not felt the upper half of the leg foundation at all. This area will be used to attach to the body.

Cover the lower half of the leg foundations with darker fiber and surface felt well to secure.

Use the twist and felt method create toes. You will need a total of 10 toes to create the two paws for the front legs.
Attach the paws to the legs.

Split the unfelted fiber of the upper leg foundations vertically. 2/3rds of the upper leg foundation will attach to the outside of the ferret body. 1/3rd of this fiber will be attached to the lower chest of the ferret.

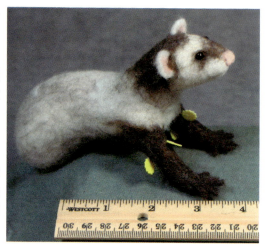

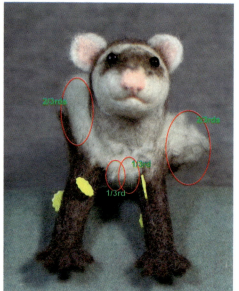

The photo on the left shows more clearly how the split, unfelted fiber of the upper legs are positioned onto the body.

Pin the front legs into place.

By splitting the upper fiber in this manner, the legs can be positioned so that they appear to be coming out of the body and not just attached to the sides.

You can alter the pose of the front legs making one farther forward than the other or evenly positioned as I have done here.

Felt the front legs to the body.

FERRET

Needle Felting – to the Point

Use core fiber to create foundations for the back legs.

I had a difficult time finding good reference photos of ferret hind legs, so I pretty much guessed at a basic shape.

Do note that there are paw stubs on these foundations.

It will be possible to refine and alter this shape.

Make toes for the back paws using the twist and felt method. I only made four toes for these paws. These paws are also longer than the front paws.

Attach the paws to the leg foundations and cover the lower half with the darker fiber.

That looks better, but there is still time for refinement.

Attach the back legs to the ferret body.

Overall, this isn't too bad, but the legs appear a bit too long and the body length still appears a bit too short.

There are several ways that such problems could be corrected. You could felt the legs into the body more firmly. This would shorten their length, but it would not lengthen the body.

You could also physically pull on the body to make it longer, but there is an easier way.

FERRET

Needle Felting – to the Point

Add core fiber to the top of the back.

Yes, eventually you will have to recover this area with the "dress" fiber, but you would have had to do that anyway.

This increased hump to the body visually increases the length of the body, but the front legs still appear to be too long.

To rectify this, add core fiber to the lower neck and chest, then taper to the tummy area.

Doing this further visually increases the length of the ferret body, at the same time making the front legs appear shorter.

When the final dress fiber is applied, the ferret will be the perfect length.

FERRET

Needle Felting – to the Point

Make a tail for the ferret about half the length of the body. I started with a twisted dark brown fiber foundation.

Pull off short lengths of fiber and felt them into the tail foundation, just as you did when making the squirrel tail.

Cover the ferret with dress fiber using dark and light and blends of the two to complete your ferret markings.

Surface felt the fiber well to secure and smooth the surface.

Nicely done!

Often when needle felting creatures, our original estimates, on quantity of fiber or the length needed, can be inaccurate.

Legs can be shortened by condensing the fiber lengthwise.

Bodies and/or legs can be lengthened by physically manipulating the piece with our hands or by adding more fiber.

The unique posture of this ferret allowed us to increase the length of the body by adding fiber to the back and under the chest. The underlying foundation did not significantly change shape, but the additional fiber increases the length by increasing the curves to the "S" shape.

The more experienced you become with needle felting the fewer major corrections you will need to make, but it is nice to know that if necessary, they're easy to make.

Needle Felting – to the Point

FAIRY – Materials Needed:
- Core Fiber
- Merino in flesh and colors for clothes and wings
- Specialty fiber for hair
- Seed beads for eyes
- Needle and thread
- Butterfly and leaf shaped cookie cutters (optional)
- Feathers (optional)

The fairy is rather small and small can be difficult.

Start by making a small, firm egg shape using carded flesh colored fiber.

The fairy head is so small that creating an egg shape from core fiber and then covering it with the flesh colored fiber is impractical.

Using a small quantity of carded flesh colored fiber, create a nose.

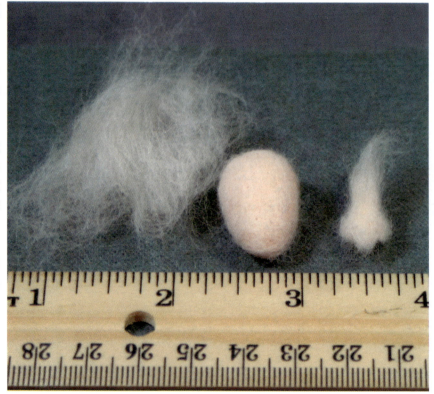

FAIRY

Needle Felting – to the Point

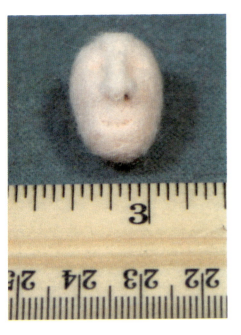

Felt the nose into place.

Using a few strands of fiber, felt shadows for the eyes and the mouth.

Use core fiber to create a torso.

The torso should be firmly felted.

Attach the head securely to the neck and cover the neck with flesh colored fiber.

The flesh fiber of the neck will also create the neckline for the fairy garment.

This fairy has a "V" neck outfit.

FAIRY

Needle Felting – to the Point

Tear off short lengths of fiber and cover the torso.

Flat felt the dress fiber securely to the core fiber foundation.

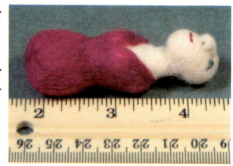

To create the legs, roll some carded fiber into a log. The rolled fiber is not firm at all.

Begin roughly shaping the log into the leg shape as seen on the photo below and to the left.

Slowly and carefully continue to reduce the fiber until it is the size of the leg in the photo below and to the right.

The finished legs are only medium firm. They are stable enough to hold their shape, but flexible enough to allow you to pose the fairy seated when she is not riding the ferret.

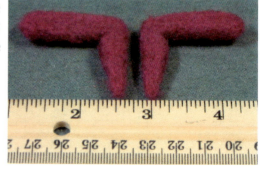

FAIRY

Needle Felting – to the Point

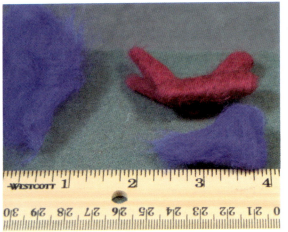

Use carded fiber, in a contrasting color to the body, to make the boots.

Start out with a roughly formed, large version of the boot and carefully reduce it in size.

Look at how large the boot looks in the photo to the left compared to the boots in the photo below!

Use scissors to snip a hole in the top of the boot into which the ankle can be inserted.

Use a needle to help you insert the ankle well into the boot.

Felt through the ankle into the bottom of the boot, and all around the ankle into the boot.

Felt through the boot sides into the ankle to further secure.

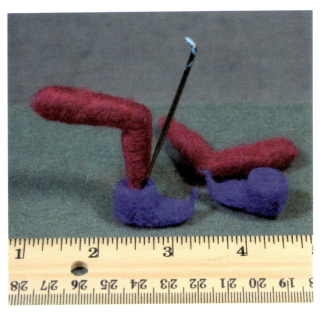

Twist felt a small thumb.

Arrange the fibers to form fingers and palm as seen in the photo to the left.

Felt from both sides.

Condense and felted the fibers to form a wrist. Gently pull away any excess fiber.

FAIRY

Make two hands.

Wrap the wrists with a small quantity of the contrasting fiber.

Felt to secure in place.

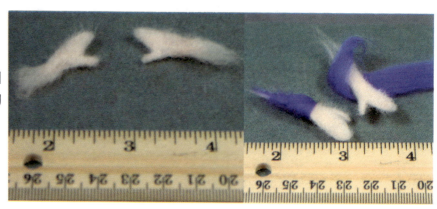

Arms are made using the same flat felting technique used to make the gnome arms.

The fairy arms require less fiber and should be, when finished, about 1" long from contrasting cuffs to finished shoulder.

Pin the fairy together to see how she is looking.

Felt the legs securely to the torso. Set the arms aside for the time being. It will be easier to add a skirt if the arms are not in the way.

FAIRY

Needle Felting – to the Point

Create a lot of leaves to make the skirt for the fairy. I used a small leaf shaped cookie cutter as a basic flat felting guide, but with variations in width and length to the leaves.

If you prefer, you could make flower petals instead of leaves, or you could use the petals from a silk flower.

You could make a skirt out of loose fibers or opt to have no skirt at all.

Attach the leaves securely to the fairy's waist.

I also made some twist felted "yarn" to detail the neckline.

Felt the arms to the fairy body at the shoulders.

Remember to felt the whole shoulder, not just the top of the sleeve.

If you want to lock the position of the arms more securely, you can tack the sleeve to the fairy body.

FAIRY

Needle Felting – to the Point

Use specialty fiber to add hair to the fairy. Shetland fiber works very well for hair. I used a fiber from a cross of Rambouillet and Icelandic sheep because I happened to have it on hand, and it was already dyed.

Shetland will work beautifully and can be dyed to whatever color you desire.

If you are going to add wings, do not arrange hair down the fairy's back.

I created the "flying ponytail" first and then attached and arranged the rest of the hair.

I used a butterfly cookie cutter to make solid colored wings. This is a simple method for flat felting a desired shape, but you can make wings without the use of a mold.

Fold the wings in half vertically and felt lightly along the fold. I added real feathers to the wings by using a small bit of fiber to felt on either side of the feather stem.

You might want to make more colorful wings, or just the plain wings without the added feathers. Felt the wings to the fairy.

FAIRY

Needle Felting – to the Point

As it happened, I ended up making the fairy twice because I had lost some photos of the step-by-step process. I made the second fairy a bit differently than the first. I'm including some photos from the first fairy because they demonstrate solving different problems.

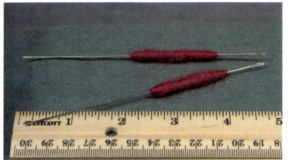

My original idea for the fairy was to give her slender arms. In preparation, I wrapped fiber around doll needles. While still on the doll needles I felted the fiber well.

I then removed the doll needles and continued to felt the fiber.

The resulting pieces were a bit too long.

It might have been possible, with considerable effort, to reduce these arms to the right size, but I opted for another solution.

Before I explain what I did do, let me explain why these arms didn't work. Wrapping fiber on doll needles does work, but the quantity of fiber for these arms was rather limited.

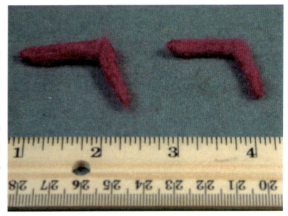

I was using Merino which has long fibers. To get wrapped Merino to felt well, you not only have to move it around with the needles, the needles need to break some of the fiber so that it can be moved further thus allowing more of the scales on the fibers to interlock.

If I had torn off short lengths of the Merino and carded it and used the carded fiber to form the arms, in the same manner I had you make the legs for the previous fairy, it would have been easier to felt and control firmness and size.

It is difficult when working on a small scale to needle felt to the "very firm" stage. If, as is likely to happen, your needles pass through the object and out the other side, you are forcing fiber out of the object as well as forcing fibers together.

This is one of the reasons many needle felters rely upon an armature to provide strength to small sculptures.

FAIRY

Needle Felting – to the Point

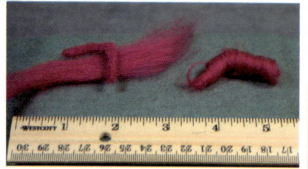

What I did was to turn the original fairy "arms" into foundations for that fairy's legs. I wrapped them with more fiber and felted them very well.

The end result was legs very similar to those I created with carded fiber.

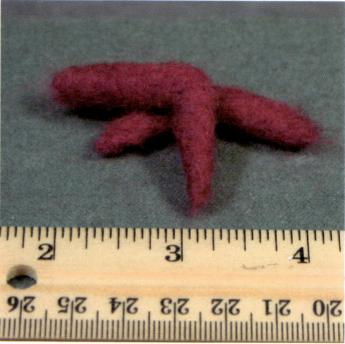

How you choose to construct your sculpture will affect how easy it is to construct and how successful will be that construction. Loose and bat fibers are closer in nature to firmly felted fiber than is drum-carded fiber. The fibers in drum-carded fiber have been aligned to run parallel to one another and well felted fibers are not aligned at all.

Tearing off short lengths of fiber and hand carding those fibers breaks the drummed alignment and begins to form the fibers into a nice tangled mess. Hand carded fiber can be more difficult to measure equally, but it is simple enough to add more fiber when needed.

Try different approaches to constructing a sculpture. They may work or they may fail, but you will learn which methods work best for you and you will learn how to turn failure into success!

Needle Felting – to the Point

WOODLAND DIORAMA:

Having created six creatures, it is time to make them a home.

Woodland Diorama – Materials Needed:
- Styrofoam Cooler (I recycled a Styrofoam cooler that came in the mail when friends had sent us some steaks)
- Craft blade or sharp knife
- Glue Gun and glue sticks
- Wire
- Wire Cutters
- Small leaf shaped cookie cutters
- Small heart shaped cookie cutter
- Fiber in many colors – I used Merino and Norwegian C1 (kiwi)
- Craft felt
- Floral tape

Felting on Styrofoam:

You can't really felt fiber to Styrofoam, but by needling your fiber into the Styrofoam at a variety of angles, you can make the fiber stick. It could, with effort, be removed.

When repeatedly pierced by felting needles, Styrofoam begins to break down.

You may notice when you begin to cover the Styrofoam with fiber (particularly the door for the tree stump) that the Styrofoam begins to feel "spongy". This is a sign that the Styrofoam is beginning to breaking down.

You want to needle enough to have the fiber stay in place, but do not over needle. I'll explain more on how to handle the door when we get to that section.

The lid of the cooler makes a good foundation for the diorama.

Not all Styrofoam is the same.

Visually it should appear dense. The Styrofoam should not melt when the hot glue (low setting) is used. Some Styrofoam can even withstand the high setting for the hot glue.

Use your craft knife to cut off one long side of the cooler.

Do not include the bottom or the corners of the cooler when removing the side.

To make pieces from which the tree stump can be formed, cut the side into 1/2th" wide slices from the top (where the lid would rest) to bottom.

WOODLAND DIORAMA

Needle Felting – to the Point

To make the construction of the tree stump easier, you will need to trim some of the strips of Styrofoam you just cut from the side.

The strips, after being cut from the side are rectangular. Trim away "V" shaped sections from the sides of the some of the strips.

How many you need to trim depends on how large you want your tree stump.

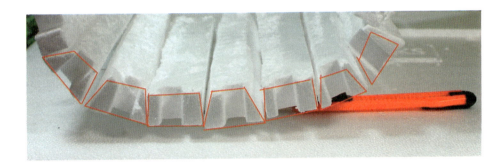

I used long pins to pin my building pieces together to get an idea of how large my stump was. Add trimmed or non-trimmed wall sections until you have your tree stump the size you want it to be.

You could make a tree stump greater in diameter than mine. If you cut the side of your cooler lengthwise, your stump could be taller and include a second floor.

Hot glue the pieces together, be sure to use the low setting.

WOODLAND DIORAMA

Do not use more glue than you need to secure the wall sections together, otherwise your needles will probably hit the excess glue and be unable to pierce it.

Use enough glue to hold the pieces together securely, but not so much that the glue becomes a problem.

When you do encounter glue, just change the angle of your felting needles.

Draw the outline for a door on the side of the tree stump that you want to face the front of the diorama.

The door should be tall enough for your Gnome. It would be a pretty sorry home for a Gnome if the door wasn't large enough for him to enter!

Carefully cut the door out of the tree stump.

Cut at a slight angle so that the inside side is slightly smaller than the outside side of the door.

By cutting at a slight angle you will ensure that the door cannot be opened or pushed into the tree stump.

Sand the edges of the door and the door opening.

Needle Felting – to the Point

You will need to sand the edges of the door and door opening to accommodate the fiber that will be used to cover both. Sanding away 1/8th" from both should work nicely.

I lined the interior of my tree stump with yellow craft felt. I really didn't want to deal with the difficulty of trying to felt fiber to the inside of the tree stump. The craft felt worked very well. You could, if you wish, decorate the craft felt before lining the interior of the tree stump.

Tear off short lengths of your door color fiber and needle it to the door as seen in the photo on the right.

The door is a limited area and you will be covering all sides. This means that you will do a lot of needling. The door will start to feel "spongy", but as long as you are careful the fiber will help to keep the Styrofoam in place. Do NOT needle all the way through the door!

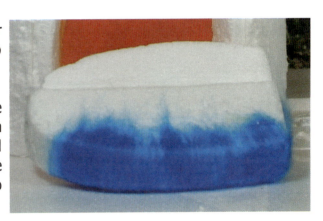

Completely cover the door with fiber.

Check to see how it fits into the door opening.

There should be enough room to be able to cover the door frame and still not put stress on the fibers of the door edges and door frame.

If your door fits too tightly, sand the door frame again.

WOODLAND DIORAMA

Needle Felting – to the Point

Decorate your door however you'd like. I added a heart and some leaves. I also felted a keyhole and used a jewelry finding as a door handle.

Cover the door frame in the same manner as you covered the sides of the door. Use thin layers of fiber to hide the Styrofoam. The fiber for the door frame should be felted in place both inside and outside the tree stump.

I created "leaf" hinges for my door. Portions of those leaves were attached first to the door and then to the door frame as seen in the photo on the left.

I cut another piece of Styrofoam from the cooler to raise the area for the tree stump.

I marked where the door is on the new piece of Styrofoam and, using the craft blade, cut steps leading to the door and contouring the edges.

So far the tree stump, new piece of Styrofoam and the lid base have not been attached to one another. We will get to that in a bit, but it is easier to work on these pieces separately.

WOODLAND DIORAMA

Needle Felting – to the Point

Cut and position a piece of craft felt to be the floor inside your tree stump.

It doesn't matter if this piece of craft felt is a little too big. It is actually easier if it is a bit larger.

Tack the craft felt to the Styrofoam, needling at different angles.

Begin covering the tree stump with core fiber.

Use core fiber to create roots and felt them to the Styrofoam.

The roots will secure the tree stump to the Styrofoam "riser", but it will not be completely secure until you have created and attached roots all the way around the base.

Do remember when you are making roots and other things for the diorama, that you will need places where your creatures can stand.

It certainly would be interesting to have a vast network of interlacing tree roots, but that would leave few areas in which to pose your creatures easily.

Note how the core fiber was applied to create a neat door frame.

WOODLAND DIORAMA

Begin covering your tree stump and roots with fiber.

I used a mix of colors blended together. Covering the stump and roots takes a lot of fiber, so you will often have to blend more. Just remember the basic proportions of colors that you used to create your "bark" blend, and you'll be fine.

Minor variations between batches of "bark" blend will not matter.

Continue to cover your tree stump and roots.

Surface felt the "bark" fiber into the core fiber below.

The core fiber should have been securely attached to the Styrofoam, so you really only need to secure the "bark" fiber to the core fiber.

It certainly will not hurt anything if you do occasionally needle into the Styrofoam.

I designed and finished my diorama so that it can be viewed from any angle.

If you intend to place your diorama on a shelf where it can only be seen from the front and sides, you don't have to finish the back.

Personally, I like knowing that all sides of my diorama are finished, even if it did mean a lot more work and a lot more fiber!

WOODLAND DIORAMA

Needle Felting – to the Point

WOODLAND DIORAMA

Needle Felting – to the Point

Once your tree stump is completely covered, use your hot glue gun (low setting) to glue the tree stump and riser to the base.

Position it carefully!

WOODLAND DIORAMA

I decided to add another piece of Styrofoam just to the left of the stairs.

This new piece was about half the height of the riser.

I had tacked roots to the riser where I decided to add this new piece, so it was necessary for me to lift up the root and a bit of the moss before gluing the new piece of Styrofoam into place.

I cut an additional step into the edge of the base and covered the path and stairs with a blend of dark browns.

Begin covering the diorama with various mixtures of greens. I used blends of Merino fiber for this first layer of "moss".

Over these areas I felted an extremely thin layer of Norwegian C1 Kiwi fiber. The Norwegian C1 has a coarser texture which, when applied thinly, allows the Merino colors to show and really looks like moss.

Needle Felting – to the Point

Now the fun really begins! There is no particular order that you need to follow when decorating the rest of the diorama.

Clover leaves can be made by using a small heart shaped cutter to flat felt three heart shapes.

Join the hearts at the point and you have a clover leaf.

Use different size hearts and you have different sized clover leaves.

Use different blends of green to add variety.

Cut wire into various lengths.

Remember to stretch the florist tape as you wrap it carefully around the wire.

Wrap the wire neatly with the floral tape, but leave at least an inch unwrapped.

WOODLAND DIORAMA

Needle Felting – to the Point

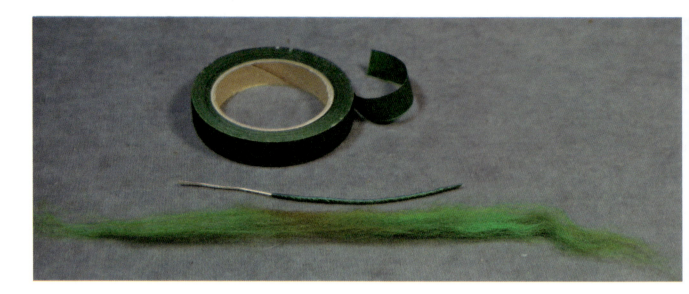

Carefully wrap a thin layer of fiber evenly onto the floral taped section of the wire.

Wire wrapped in this manner will be used for stems for plants.

It takes a bit of practice to learn to do this neatly, but even your first attempts will be useful!

When you come to the end of the floral tape, wrap the fiber around two or three times and felt with your needles to secure the fiber in place.

Trim away excess fiber. Felt the bottom very well and remember to rotate the stem while felting.

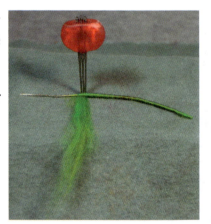

Instead of trimming the excess fiber, you can twist felt the excess fiber to become a leaf or a limp blade of grass.

You could also flat felt the excess fiber to form a wider leaf.

You could add fiber to have greater control over the shape.

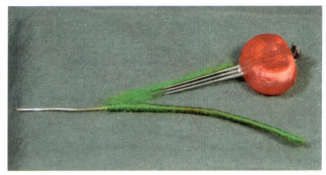

These stems are useful as pictured here, and they can be modified to give you a wide variety of foliage.

Ferns can be created by making matching sets of leaves and felting them opposite one another on the fiber covered stem.

I used this metal cutter as a mold to help form these leaves more quickly, but it isn't necessary; you could also flat felt such leaves without a mold.

WOODLAND DIORAMA

Needle Felting – to the Point

Create a totally different plant by creating leaves of a different shape and felting them to the stem in different patterns and/or density.

There are endless possibilities!

To add these plants to your diorama, use your wire cutters to cut the uncovered wire end into a point and stick it through the moss into the Styrofoam.

Twist felt fiber to create vines.

Pin the vines to your tree stump to arrange them nicely and then felt to secure them to the tree stump.

WOODLAND DIORAMA

Needle Felting – to the Point

Create leaves for your vine.

I used a small cutter as a flat felt mold to make these leaves. Although they could be made without one, it is easier to use a mold.

I used a variety of greens for my leaves and I also varied the shapes and sizes to give a more natural appearance.

You can twist felt, or felt fiber wrapped on doll needles to create long thin logs that can be rolled and felted together to form fiddlehead ferns.

Fiddleheads are just felted into place wherever you may want them on the diorama.

Twist and felt different blends of green fibers in varying lengths to make tiny blades of grass.

Roll the felted portion firmly between palm and finger to smooth the surface.

Hold the tip of these blades of grass when felting the feathered bottom fiber into the diorama.

WOODLAND DIORAMA

Needle Felting – to the Point

Blended fiber can be felted into a variety of shapes.

If you want complete control over the position of the larger leaves, you might felt a wire down the middle.

Many leaves like this could be used to create a Bird Nest Fern.

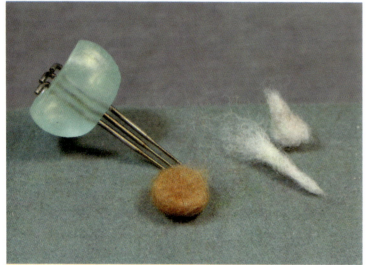

You can twist felt fat or thick, long or short stems for mushrooms.

WOODLAND DIORAMA

Needle Felting – to the Point

Felt all around the stem to secure it firmly to the mushroom cap.

Flowers can also be made starting with twist and felt stems. I used small molds to quickly felt the petals.

Use core fiber to roughly shape rocks.

WOODLAND DIORAMA

Needle Felting – to the Point

Cover with colored fiber.

Continue to refine the shape and add some moss to the rocks as a finishing touch.

Finish covering the diorama foundation with moss.

I found it easier to make a lot of the different items, grass, mushrooms, flowers, ferns, etc. and then to decorate one specific area of the diorama.

Again, keep in mind that you will need places for your creatures to stand so not all areas should be heavily decorated.

Creatures can stand on leaves.

WOODLAND DIORAMA

Although both time and fiber consuming, dioramas are not difficult to make. You're certainly not limited to making a tree stump home. You are also not limited to the size of a Styrofoam cooler lid. You could use a piece of plywood in whatever size you desired for the base. Glue Styrofoam to your plywood and make whatever you want!

You could make a cave, or a village of Gnome homes or you could make .....

Needle Felting – to the Point

... a restful waterfall.

You're also not limited to only using needle felted elements. As you can see, this artificial bonsai tree works quite well in this scene.

The river was needle felted on craft felt and then inserted into this diorama. The waterfalls were created by using a thin layer of white fiber felted at the top, draped to look like water falling, and the ends condensed and lightly felted into the splash at the bottom.

Needle Felting – to the Point

Favorite Resources:

Mielke's Fiber Arts, LLC **Rudolph, WI 54475** http://www.mielkesfarm.com/index.htm	A great source for fibers and excellent prices!!
Frankenmuth Woolen Mill http://www.thewoolenmill.com/	Super source for core fiber! Sold as batting for quilts a crib size provides a lot of core fiber for a lot of projects! Sometimes contains some vegetable matter but still the best core fiber I have used!
Van Dykes Taxidermy **P.O. Box 367** **Woonsocket, SD 57385** http://www.vandykestaxidermy.com/	Great glass eyes in a wide variety of sizes!

Find me on Flickr at: http://www.flickr.com/photos/prittens/

Visit my oil painting website at: http://www.intimtateforest.com/

Like me on FaceBook: http://www.facebook.com/pages/Harlan/133295863359168

Take online and on demand classes at: http://www.craftedu.com/

Needle Felting – to the Point

Bark 92
Boot 79
Clover leaves 97
Color, running out of 25
Correcting Length 18
Detail 13, 16, 81
Door 85
Dyeing Wool 56
Ears 34, 38, 50, 59, 71
Fairy 76
Ferns 99
Ferret 67
Firmness 5, 9
Flat felt 29
Flowers 103
Frog 40
Gnome 56
Grass 99, 101, 104
Hands 4, 61, 75, 80
Leaves 81, 90, 97, 99, 100, 101, 102, 104
Moss 96
Moving fiber 22
Mushrooms 102
Nose 32, 34, 43, 45, 46, 48, 57, 58, 67, 68, 69, 76, 77
Paws 32, 38, 39, 53, 54, 55, 72, 73
Rocks 103
Size 5
Sleeves 61, 62
Twist felt 35
Vines 100
Winged Mouse 30
Woodland Diorama 85

Made in the USA
San Bernardino, CA
15 May 2014